An I Can Read Book®

# More Surprises

selected by Lee Bennett Hopkins

illustrated by Megan Lloyd

A CHARLOTTE ZOLOTOW BOOK

Harper & Row, Publishers

1           of

Harper & Row, Publishers, Inc.

*Library of Congress Cataloging-in-Publication Data*
Hopkins, Lee Bennett.
  More surprises.

  (An I can read book)
  "A Charlotte Zolotow book."
  Summary: A collection of poems with topics ranging
from school to birds to nonsense.
  1. Children's poetry, American.  [1. American
poetry—Collections]  I. Lloyd, Megan, ill.  II. Title.
III. Series.
PS586.3.H66  1987      811'.008'09282      86-45335
ISBN 0-06-022604-8
ISBN 0-06-022605-6 (lib. bdg.)

## Acknowledgments

Every effort has been made to trace the ownership of all copyrighted material and to
secure the necessary permissions to reprint these selections. In the event of any question
arising as to the use of any material, the editor and publisher, while expressing regret for
any inadvertent error, will be happy to make the necessary correction in future printings.
Thanks are due to the following for permission to reprint the copyrighted materials listed
below:

Atheneum Publishers, Inc. for "Ruth Luce and Bruce Booth" and "Lion" from *Snowman
Sniffles* by N. M. Bodecker. Copyright © 1982 by N. M. Bodecker (A Margaret K.

2

Moore Publishing Company, Durham, North Carolina, for "An Historic Moment" and "On Wearing Ears" by William J. Harris from *Nine Black Poets*.

Sara Perkins for "Worm." Used by permission of the author, who controls all rights.

The Putnam Publishing Group for "My Nose" from *All Together* by Dorothy Aldis. Copyright 1925–1928, 1934, 1939, 1952, copyright renewed 1953–1956, 1962, 1967 by Dorothy Aldis. Reprinted by permission of G. P. Putnam's Sons.

Marian Reiner for "Picture People" from *Whispers and Other Poems* by Myra Cohn Livingston. Copyright © 1958 by Myra Cohn Livingston. Reprinted by permission of Marian Reiner for the author.

Marci Ridlon for "Open Hydrant." Used by permission of the author, who controls all rights.

Viking Penguin Inc. for "Brother" from *Yellow Butter Purple Jelly Red Jam Black Bread* by Mary Ann Hoberman. Copyright © 1981 by Mary Ann Hoberman. Reprinted by permission of Viking Penguin Inc.

Charlotte Zolotow for "People" from *All That Sunlight* (Harper & Row, Publishers, Inc.). Used by permission of the author, who controls all rights.

To Misha Arenstein—
Teacher. Friend.
LBH

For Jack and Jean, surprise!
ML

# Some People

# People

Charlotte Zolotow

Some people talk and talk

and never say a thing.

Some people look at you

and birds begin to sing.


Some people laugh and laugh

and yet you want to cry.

Some people touch your hand

and music fills the sky.

7

## Brother

Mary Ann Hoberman

I had a little brother

And I brought him to my mother

And I said I want another

Little brother for a change.

But she said don't be a bother

So I took him to my father

And I said this little bother

Of a brother's very strange.

8

But he said one little brother

Is exactly like another

And every little brother

Misbehaves a bit, he said.

So I took the little bother

From my mother and my father

And I put the little bother

Of a brother back to bed.

9

# Mary Ann the Witch Girl

Pamela Espeland and Marilyn Waniek

Mary Ann the witch girl

Sneaks out at night

Closes the screen door

Locks it up tight

Faces the apple tree

Turns toward the house

10

Whispers a magic spell

Squeaks like a mouse

Chooses a special star

Then makes two wishes...


And passes arithmetic

And NEVER does dishes!

11

## An Historic Moment

William J. Harris

The man said,

after inventing poetry,

"WOW!"

and did a full somersault.

12

# The Question

Karla Kuskin

People always say to me

"What do you think you'd like to be

When you grow up?"

And I say "Why,

I think I'd like to be the sky

Or be a plane or train or mouse

Or maybe be a haunted house

Or something furry, rough and wild...

Or maybe I will stay a child."

13

# Body Parts

# On Wearing Ears

William J. Harris

As long as people

continue to wear

ears

there won't

be much

peace and quiet

in this world.

# My Nose

Dorothy Aldis

It doesn't breathe;

It doesn't smell;

It doesn't feel

So very well.

I am discouraged

With my nose:

The only thing it

Does is blows.

17

## Whistling

Jack Prelutsky

Oh, I can laugh and I can sing

and I can scream and shout,

but when I try to whistle,

the whistle won't come out.

18

I shape my lips the proper way,

I make them small and round,

but when I blow, just air comes out,

there is no whistling sound.

But I'll keep trying very hard

to whistle loud and clear,

and someday soon I'll whistle tunes

for everyone to hear.

# This Tooth

Lee Bennett Hopkins

I jiggled it

    jaggled it

    jerked it.

I pushed

    and pulled

    and poked it.

20

But—

As soon as I stopped,

and left it alone,

This tooth came out

on its very own!

## Ruth Luce and Bruce Booth

N. M. Bodecker

Said little Ruth Luce

to little Bruce Booth:

"Lithen," said Ruth

"I've a little looth tooth!"


Said little Bruce Booth:

"Tho what if you do?

that'th nothing thpethial—

I've a looth tooth too!"

## Toes

Victoria Forrester

The baby's toes...

I could put them in my mouth

Like spring vegetables.

23

# Living Things

# The Caterpillar

Christina G. Rossetti

Brown and furry

Caterpillar in a hurry;

Take your walk

To the shady leaf or stalk.


May no toad spy you,

May the little birds pass by you;

Spin and die,

To live again a butterfly.

# I Talk With the Moon

Beverly McLoughland

I talk with the moon, said the owl

While she lingers over my tree

I talk with the moon, said the owl

And the night belongs to me.

26

I talk with the sun, said the wren

As soon as he starts to shine

I talk with the sun, said the wren

And the day is mine.

# from
# Something Sleeping in the Hall

Karla Kuskin

My bird is small.

My bird is shy.

It does not sing.

It cannot fly.

It does no tricks

and that is fine.

I love my bird.

My bird is mine.

28

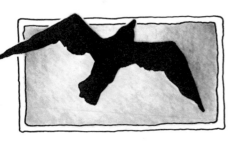

# Sea Gull

Elizabeth Coatsworth

The sea gull curves his wings,

the sea gull turns his eyes.

Get down in the water, fish!

(if you are wise.)


The sea gull slants his wings,

the sea gull turns his head.

Get deep into the water, fish!

(or you'll be dead.)

29

## Lion

N. M. Bodecker

The lion,

when he roars

at night,

gives many people

quite

a fright!

The lion,

when he roars

by day,

scares people near him

far

away.

And when

he sleeps,

his lion snore

is quite as scary as

his

roar.

# How
# Funny

# Going Out One Day

Anonymous

As I was going out one day,

My head fell off and rolled away.

But when I saw that it was gone,

I picked it up and put it on.

And when I went into the street,

A fellow cried, "Look at your feet!"

I looked at them and sadly said,

"I've left them both asleep in bed!"

## Who Ever Sausage a Thing?

Anonymous

One day a boy went walking

And went into a store;

He bought a pound of sausages

And laid them on the floor.

34

The boy began to whistle

A merry little tune—

And all the little sausages

Danced around the room!

# A Young Farmer of Leeds

Anonymous

There was a young farmer of Leeds

Who swallowed six packets of seeds.

It soon came to pass

He was covered with grass

And he could not sit down

For the weeds.

36

# The Boy Stood on the Burning Deck

Anonymous

The boy stood on the burning deck

Eating peanuts by the peck;

His father called him,

He would not go,

Because he loved his peanuts so.


The boy stood on the burning deck

His feet were full of blisters;

The flames came up

And burned his pants

And now he wears his sister's.

## Worm

Sara Perkins

The worm in the apple

rests in his chair.

He's nibbled his rooftop

and eaten his stairs.

He's gnawed off his kitchen,

the chimney's not there.

When his front porch is swallowed,

he'll go on to pears.

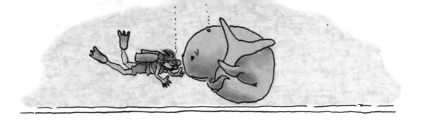

# If You Ever Meet a Whale

Anonymous

If you ever, ever, ever, ever,

ever meet a whale,

You must never, never,

never, never

grab him by his tail.

If you ever, ever, ever, ever

grab him by his tail—

You will never, never,

never, never

meet another whale.

# The Witch's Song

Lilian Moore

Hey! Cackle! Hey!

Let's have fun today.

All shoelaces will have knots.

No knots will untie.

Every glass of milk will spill.

Nothing wet will dry.

Every pencil point will break.

And everywhere in town

Peanut-buttered bread will drop

Upside down.

Hey! Hey! Hey!

Have a pleasant day.

# Hot and Cold

# In July

Sandra Liatsos

If only my street

were under the sea

and I were a dolphin

as cool as can be,

swimming and diving

and having my fun

down in the wetness

away from the sun.

# Open Hydrant

Marci Ridlon

Water rushes up

and gushes,

cooling summer's sizzle.


In a sudden whoosh

it rushes,

not a little drizzle.

First a hush and down

it crashes,

over curbs it swishes.

Just a luscious waterfall

for

cooling city fishes.

## No

William Cole

No birds, no flowers,

No sunshiny hours,

No days without rain

Or frost on the pane;

No fresh fruit is sold,

No weather but cold—

Please, Nature, remember:

Next year, skip November!

## A Season

Lillian M. Fisher

First snow

   falling,

Wild geese

   calling.

Fields

   bare,

Winter

   whispers

      everywhere.

# I Do Not Mind You, Winter Wind

Jack Prelutsky

I do not mind you, Winter Wind

when you come whirling by,

to tickle me with snowflakes

drifting softly from the sky.

I do not even mind you

when you nibble at my skin,

scrambling over all of me

attempting to get in.

48

But when you bowl me over

and I land on my behind,

then I must tell you, Winter Wind,

I mind...I really mind!

49

## Signs of the Seasons

Anonymous

A winter sled.

A book read.

An April shower.

A spring flower.

50

A summer day.

A child at play.

Autumn.


Then—

It is winter again.

# In School and After

# Back to School

Aileen Fisher

When summer smells like apples

and shadows feel cool

and falling leaves make dapples

of color on the pool

and wind is in the maples

and sweaters are the rule

and hazy days spell lazy ways,

it's hard to go to school.


But I go!

# Writing on the Chalkboard

Isabel Joshlin Glaser

Up and down, my chalk goes.

*Squeak, squeak, squeak!*

Hush, chalk.

Don't squawk.

Talk *softly* when you speak.

## School Concert

Marchette Chute

My family was the very proudest.

They said my singing was the loudest.

# Good Books, Good Times!

Lee Bennett Hopkins

Good books.

Good times.

Good stories.

Good rhymes.

Good beginnings.

Good ends.

Good people.

Good friends.

Good fiction.

Good facts.

Good adventures.

Good acts.

Good stories.

Good rhymes.

*Good* books.

*Good* times.

# Picture People

Myra Cohn Livingston

I like to peek

inside a book

where all the picture people look.

I like to peek

at them and see

if they are peeking back at me.

# Keep a Poem in Your Pocket

Beatrice Schenk de Regniers

Keep a poem in your pocket

and a picture in your head

and you'll never feel lonely

at night when you're in bed.


The little poem will sing to you

the little picture bring to you

a dozen dreams to dance to you

at night when you're in bed.

60

So—

Keep a picture in your pocket

and a poem in your head

and you'll never feel lonely

at night when you're in bed.

61

# Index of Authors and Titles

63

Detroit City Ordinance 29-85, Section
29-2-2(b) provides: "Any person who
retains any library material or any part
thereof for more than fifty (50) cal-
endar days beyond the due date shall be
guilty of a misdemeanor."

The number of books that may be
drawn at one time by the card holder is
governed by the reasonable needs of the
reader and the material on hand.

Books for junior readers are subject
to special rules.

MAR '88